SUCCESS BLUEPRINT: FOR IIT-JEE AND NEET

Dr. Balraju Karri

(B. Tech. NIT WARANGAL)
Award Winning Coach and Entrepreneur
International Author, Motivational Speaker

*This book is dedicated to the guiding lights of my life—those whose wisdom,
love, and unwavering support have shaped my journey.
To my Spiritual Guru,* **HH Radhanath Swami;**
my Spiritual Siksha Gurus, **HG Radheshyam Das** *and*
HG Sundershyam Das;
my Business Coach, **Dr. Ameet Parekh;**
my beloved Father, **Apparao Karri;**
my dear Mother, **Bhavani Karri;**
and my supportive Wife, **Monika Karri**—*thank you for being my strength.*

*This book is for you, the unsung heroes of education,
who transform challenges into stepping stones toward success.
May these pages inspire every student to rise, dream big, and conquer their future.*

CONTENTS

PREFACE

I wrote this book to help every student in India preparing for competitive exams like JEE and NEET. Even those tackling state-level entrances such as EAMCET, KCET, WBJEE, MHCET, and others can benefit 100% from this guide. Over the past 15 years, I have mentored countless students—some soared to success, some faced setbacks, and many came very close. Each experience has deepened my understanding of the challenges students face and the common mindsets that hold them back.

I have learned countless lessons from my own journey. I was selected at NIT Warangal through sheer determination, even when many of my relatives doubted my potential. I struggled with public speaking and speaking English in college, yet I worked hard to transform these challenges into strengths. Over time, I evolved into a faculty member, a business owner who has helped many students secure seats in IITs, NITs, and government medical colleges, and ultimately, a motivational speaker and author. After COVID, I further invested in my personal growth with guidance from masterminds like Brian Tracy, Robin Sharma, Dr. Ameet Parekh, and Dr. Vivek Bindra. I learned from top authors, international coaches, my spiritual gurus, and my own life experiences. Through it all, I discovered that the right mindset is the foundation upon which every skill is built.

I wanted to share all my learnings and wisdom with every sincere student preparing to fulfill their dreams—not just to earn big salaries, but to add value to society and our nation. Many students invest lakhs in coaching classes, yet some make the wrong choices, while others follow the right path but lack the proper strategy or mindset. This often leads to wasted time, energy, and money, and ultimately, to failure.

In these pages, I share what I believe is the winning formula: how to choose the right coaching institute, adopt effective study strategies, build essential habits, and develop a success mindset. I also draw on lessons from scriptures, legends, and my own journey to offer you practical insights that can transform your life.

Every challenge you face on this demanding journey is addressed here with clear, practical solutions you can use right away. Although this book is designed mainly for JEE and NEET aspirants, the principles of mindset and strategy apply to every student. I truly believe that if you follow this guide and remain committed, success is not just a possibility—it's a guarantee.

I would like to express my heartfelt gratitude to all the students who have enriched my life with their diverse experiences. A special thank you to my wife, Monika Karri, for supporting me unconditionally and allowing me to devote myself to this effort. I am also deeply grateful for the prayers and blessings of my Spiritual Gurus, coaches, family, friends, and staff.

Welcome to your journey of transformation. Let's build the future you deserve—together.

CHAPTER 1

WELCOME TO THE BATTLEFIELD OF DREAMS: YOUR WAR TO WIN

Imagine stepping into a place where millions are competing, yet only a select few come out on top. Every year, a huge number of students set their sights on exams like JEE and NEET, each one dreaming of that coveted seat. But here's a reality check:

⇒ There are only a limited number of government MBBS seats available.

⇒ Only a small fraction of seats in government BAMS programs open the door to careers in Ayurveda.

⇒ Similarly, government BDS seats are few for those aiming to become top dental professionals.

⇒ In the engineering world, only a modest number of seats exist across top institutes like IITs and NITs.

⇒ Even in emerging institutions like IIITs, the spots are limited.

The stark contrast? Seats are in the thousands, while students number in the lakhs

Thousands of coaching classes churn out vast numbers of students, leading to cut-throat competition. The truth is, the competition isn't just tough—it's ruthless. But before you worry too much, let me share something important:

You're Not Here to Be a Statistic

You're here because you want to be one of the winners. And that means it's time to change the way you think.

This Is Your War to Win

If you believe that cracking JEE or NEET is all about studying hard, think again. It's a test of endurance, discipline, and focus. Success isn't just about hitting the books—it's about transforming your lifestyle to match your big dreams. Here's what needs to change right away:

⇒ **No more time waste:** In Parties, weddings, or picnics. Enjoyment now might cost you success later.

⇒ **Attend every class:** Skipping lectures or procrastinating only puts you a step behind.

⇒ **Get your sleep right:** Your brain needs proper rest to perform at its best.

⇒ **Cut the distractions:** That means limiting your time on mobile phones, social media, and even unnecessary relationships.

A Simple Truth

If you're not willing to make sacrifices, someone else will grab your dream. But if you're truly ready to commit, welcome to one of the most transformative journeys of your life. The road ahead is challenging, but the rewards will change your life.

So, are you ready to fight for your future?

CHAPTER 2

CHOOSING THE RIGHT COACHING INSTITUTE: YOUR FUTURE DEPENDS ON IT

Imagine standing at a crossroads with dozens of signboards, each claiming to lead you to success. Welcome to the world of coaching institutes—where marketing is king, and reality is often hidden behind flashy advertisements.

Every year, thousands of students and parents fall into the trap of misleading results, fake success stories, and overhyped claims. Some coaching centers thrive on sheer volume—enrolling thousands, knowing that a handful will succeed by probability, not by their efforts.

So how do you separate fact from fiction?

How do you find an institute that truly cares about your success, not just their profits?

The 7 Key Parameters to Choose the Right Coaching Institute

Before investing your future and your parents' hard-earned money, evaluate the institute based on these seven crucial factors:

1. Age & Reputation of the Coaching Center

⇒ Certainly a good brand has proved its quality but still you need to check the quality of it locally as it may not have same quality everywhere.

⇒ Ask locally. How many years has this specific center been running?

⇒ Enquire in the surrounding, whether the reputation is good?

⇒ Talk to serious students who are studying in that coaching center. You will get a genuine feedback from serious and sincere students.

2. Previous Results – The Truth Behind the Toppers

⇒ Beware of deceptive marketing! Many institutes showcase all-India toppers to attract admissions, even if those students studied at a different branch or sometimes they are 100% fake.

⇒ Ask for **local** results. How many students from this specific center cracked JEE/NEET in the last few years?

⇒ Verify results randomly. Ask their contact details from center and talk to one or two students if possible. (Note: Do this only if you are really unsure of their results)

3. Faculty Experience – The Backbone of Learning

⇒ Would you trust a fresher to teach you how to drive? Then why trust an inexperienced teacher with your future?

⇒ Look for **5-10 years of experience** in JEE/NEET coaching if they are not IITians/NITians

⇒ IITians/NITians as faculty? They may teach well even with lesser experience since they've personally gone through the process.

4. Doubt-Solving System – A Make-or-Break Factor

⇒ What happens when you don't understand a topic? Do you get personal attention, or are you left struggling?

⇒ Can you ask the teacher directly, or are you redirected to assistants?

⇒ Is there a system for **relearning** topics you didn't understand in class?

⇒ Some institutes ignore weak students and focus only on toppers. **Don't get sidelined!**

5. Motivation & Personal Guidance – More Important Than You Think

⇒ JEE/NEET is a **mental battle** as much as an academic one.

⇒ Does the institute provide **regular motivation** to keep you on track?

⇒ Are there mentorship sessions, personal guidance, or motivational talks to help you stay focused?

⇒ The right guidance at the right time can save your career.

6. Demo Classes – The Ultimate Test Before You Pay

⇒ **Never pay full fees upfront!**

⇒ Take a **1-week free demo class** to evaluate:

⇒ Are the teachers clear, engaging, and effective?

⇒ Are your doubts being addressed properly?

⇒ Are you comfortable with the teaching style?

⇒ Some institutes refuse demo classes because they fear students won't join after experiencing the reality. If needed, pay a small token amount (₹5000) and commit the rest later. **Losing ₹5000 is better than wasting two years in the wrong place.**

7. The Intent of the Owner – Passion or Just Business?

⇒ Who runs the institute? The owner's vision determines the entire culture of the coaching center.

⇒ Is the owner **passionate about student success** or only focused on money making?

⇒ Do they care for **all students equally**, or do they ignore the average ones and focus on few toppers ?

⇒ Owner or Franchise holder himself must be good teacher and an expert strategy maker.

Final Thought – Choose Wisely, It's Your Future!

A bad coaching decision can waste **precious years, money,energy and even your dreams.**

But the right choice can be **the launchpad to your success.**

Don't fall for the hype.

Do your research.

And remember—**no coaching institute can guarantee your success. Only YOU can.**

CHAPTER 3

VALUE OVER COST: THE SMART WAY TO CHOOSE A COACHING INSTITUTE

When it comes to education, most parents unknowingly ask the wrong question-"**What is the fee?**" Instead, they should be asking, "**What value does this institute provide?**"

Different parents have different approaches when choosing a coaching institute:

⇒ Some look for the **cheapest** option, assuming all institutes teach the same.

⇒ Some chase **big brand names**, believing popularity guarantees success.

⇒ Some prefer **premium coaching centers**, thinking high fees mean high quality.

But neither price nor brand name should be the deciding factor. The real question is: **Does the institute truly care about the success of every student, or just want to fill the admissions for Vitamin M (Money)?**

The Right Approach: Value Before Fee

Before enrolling your child, take a step back and evaluate what you're really paying for. A coaching institute is not just about lectures—it's about **guidance, mentorship, strategy, and support. It a not a tuition center, rather a coaching center. They are not supposed to say do the smart work but guide the students how to do smart work?**

What to do ? Everyone knows it. But coaching center should teach – How to do?

Few key parameters that you can check apart from what we discussed in chapter 2 which will help you make a better decision.

Key Parameters to Evaluate a Coaching Institute

⇒ **Quality of Study Material:** Are the books and notes well-researched, exam-oriented, and easy to understand?

⇒ **Faculty Expertise:** Are the teachers experienced and passionate? Are they invested in student success? Are they full time ? Available for your doubts and concerns?

⇒ **Study Mentors & Career Guidance:** Does the institute provide **personal mentors** who guide students academically and emotionally?

⇒ **Ownership & Leadership:** Are the directors truly educators or just businesspeople? Are they actively involved in shaping the learning experience? Do the leaders interact with students? Are they themselves have cracked these exams or have a vast experience of it ?

⇒ **Doubt Clearance Support:** What is systems for clearing the doubts of students? Are the students encouraged for same? How effective is the doubt –solving system? Do you see suitable for yourself?

⇒ **Support for Sincere and Average Students:** Does the institute focus only on toppers, or does it put in **extra effort for struggling students?** What provisions they have? Ask strategy, not philosophy.

⇒ **Value Education & Mindset Development:** Does the institute only focus on academics, or does it also help in **mental strength, motivation, and character-building?**

⇒ **Study Room & Facilities:** Does the institute provide a distraction-free **study environment** to help students focus?

The Fee-Value Comparison: Think Before You Decide

Let's compare different types of coaching institutes:

1. The "Hyped" Coaching Center (Expensive but Selective)

⇒ Charges hefty fees but focuses only on students who can bring **all-India ranks.**

⇒ Other students are neglected, receiving little to no personalized guidance.

⇒ No dedicated support system to uplift struggling students.

⇒ **End result:** Some rankers emerge, but the majority feel lost and left behind.

2. The "Budget" Coaching Center (Low Fee, Low Value)

⇒ Offers education at a low cost but compromises on faculty or resources or support system.

⇒ Doubt-solving is weak or non-existent, leaving students confused.

⇒ No structured progress tracking, leading to inefficient learning.

⇒ **End result:** Money saved initially, but future opportunities lost and have to spend 10 times more later

3. The "Value-Driven" Institute (Balanced & Student-Centric)

⇒ Focuses on **every student,** not just the top 1%.

⇒ Provides **personalized mentorship, career guidance,** and **systematic doubt-solving sessions.**

⇒ Tracks progress and ensures **each student is prepared** for some entrance exam, even if not JEE/NEET.

⇒ **End result:** Students gain clarity, confidence, and a real chance at success.

Smart Investments Pay Off

Think of it this way:

⇒ **Would you buy the cheapest car** without checking its safety and reliability?

⇒ **Would you choose a doctor** based only on the lowest consultation fee?

⇒ Then **why compromise on education,** which is the foundation of your child's future?

Some parents focus on cost, some on branding, some on exclusivity—but the best approach is to **analyze the value being offered, not just the fee.**

Education is not an expense—it's an investment. And just like any good investment, you must evaluate:

⇒ **What returns will it provide?**

⇒ **Is the quality worth the cost?**

⇒ **What do past students and parents say about it?**

⇒ **Does it align with my child's goal?**

Final Thought: Choose Wisely

The right coaching should **uplift every student, not just the toppers.** Instead of focusing on **finding the lowest fee or the most hyped brand,** focus on finding the institute that provides the highest value for every student.

A smart investment in education today ensures a lifetime of opportunities tomorrow. Choose wisely!

CHAPTER 4

MASTER THE BASICS – MAKE YOUR JOURNEY SMOOTHER

Imagine building a skyscraper on weak soil. No matter how grand it looks, it will eventually collapse. The same applies to JEE/NEET preparation. Even with the best coaching, the best books, and hours of study, success will remain out of reach if the foundation is weak.

Do you know know,most people say JEE and NEET means you have to go deep. What is the meaning of this ? Most often students misinterpret it to be solving more difficult problems or having higher knowledge etc. But just think ! If I tell you go deeper wherever you are standing right now. What you will find is the foundation of your house. That means more your fundamentals are stronger- easier to understand any topic of JEE and NEET. More your basics are weak, more it will be difficult for you to understand the topics of JEE and NEET.

Before jumping into complex problem-solving, an important question must be asked: **Is the foundation strong enough to support the journey ahead?**

Why Mastering Basics is Non–Negotiable

Some students begin their preparation as early as 6th or 8th grade, attending foundation courses that give them a head start. By the time they enter 11th grade, they have already developed a strong conceptual grip, making their JEE/NEET journey smoother and less stressful.

However, many students decide to pursue JEE or NEET only after 10th grade. While this may seem like a disadvantage, it is not. The key is to act immediately. The sooner the basics are strengthened, the easier and more effective the preparation becomes.

How to Identify and Strengthen the Basics

If You've Already Joined a Coaching Institute

⇒ A good coaching institute provides a structured foundation course (if chosen wisely—refer to Chapter 2 and 3).

⇒ Follow the institute's guidance diligently, as they know exactly what fundamental concepts need reinforcement.

⇒ Don't just attend lectures—revise and practice fundamental topics regularly.

⇒ Use doubt-solving sessions effectively to clear even the smallest conceptual gaps.

If You Haven't Chosen a Coaching Yet

⇒ **Ask Your School Teachers** – Request a list of essential concepts to master before starting JEE/NEET preparation.

⇒ **Use AI-Based Learning Platforms** – Tools like ChatGPT can help with topic recommendations, important concepts, and study resources.

⇒ **Connect with Seniors** – Reach out to students who have successfully cleared JEE/NEET for guidance on what matters most.

⇒ **Self-Study with the Right Resources** – Invest in foundation-level books from reputed coaching institutes or publishers.

The Danger of Ignoring the Basics

Many students fall into the trap of skipping foundational learning and jumping straight into JEE/NEET-level problems. This might seem like a shortcut, but it leads to serious problems later.

⇒ **Lack of Conceptual Clarity** – Memorizing formulas without understanding concepts results in failure when facing application-based or tricky questions.

⇒ **Struggles with Advanced Topics** – Higher-level problems require a strong grasp of fundamentals; without it, students waste time trying to decode complex questions.

⇒ **Increased Stress and Burnout** – The frustration of not being able to solve problems despite hours of effort can lead to anxiety, demotivation, and burnout.

Final Thoughts: Invest in the Basics Today for a Stronger Tomorrow

A strong foundation today prevents unnecessary struggles tomorrow. Every minute spent reinforcing fundamentals now will save countless hours of confusion and revision later.

JEE/NEET preparation is not just about solving difficult questions—it's about **clarity, confidence, and consistency**. Those who take the time to strengthen their basics today will find themselves on a much smoother and more successful path to their goal.

CHAPTER 5

3 HABITS TO BECOME AVENGER OF YOUR OWN JOURNEY

Your habits shape your success and empower you to overcome every obstacle on your journey. If you dream of cracking JEE or NEET, it's not just about hard work—it's about working smart. And real smartness comes from small but powerful habits that transform your mindset, focus, and efficiency. Let's skip the usual advice and dive straight into three high-impact habits that can turn you into the Avenger of your own journey.

1. Waking Up Early – The Ultimate Brain Hack

Ever noticed how your mind feels clearer in the morning? There's a reason for that.

🧠 **Imagine your brain as a cup:**

⇒ In the early morning, the cup is empty, ready to absorb fresh knowledge.

⇒ At night, it's already overflowing with thoughts, distractions, and fatigue.

So, when do you think learning is most effective? Obviously, in the morning!

💡 **How to Become a Morning Person: Unlock Your Peak Productivity Hours**

Most people struggle with waking up early, even though they know it's beneficial. The secret? Small, gradual changes—not sudden, extreme shifts.

The 15-Minute Rule: Transform Your Mornings Step by Step

If you usually wake up at 7 AM, don't force yourself to wake up at 4 AM overnight. Instead:

- ⇒ **Week 1:** Wake up at 6:45 AM (just 15 minutes earlier).
- ⇒ **Week 2:** Wake up at 6:30 AM.
- ⇒ **Week 3:** Wake up at 6:15 AM.
- ⇒ **Week 4:** Wake up at 6:00 AM … and so on.

Within 2-3 months, you'll comfortably reach an early start—without feeling exhausted!

Benefits of Studying During Brahma Muhurta (Early Mornings)

- ⇒ **Enhanced Mental Clarity:** The quiet and peaceful environment helps you absorb and process information more efficiently.
- ⇒ **Deep Concentration:** With minimal distractions, your focus is sharper, making study sessions more productive.
- ⇒ **Spiritual Connection:** Many find that this time fosters inner calm and strengthens their spiritual well-being, which in turn boosts overall confidence and stress management.
- ⇒ **Increased Energy:** Starting your day with a clear mind sets a positive tone, energizing you for the challenges ahead.

Real-Life Example: The Success Formula of APJ Abdul Kalam

Dr. A.P.J. Abdul Kalam, India's "Missile Man," was known for his disciplined morning routine. He would wake up before sunrise, meditate, and read scriptures before starting his day. This habit gave him laser-sharp focus and allowed him to contribute tirelessly to India's scientific advancements.

💡 **Lesson:** If a scientist managing critical national projects could find time for early mornings, so can you!

2. Early & Light Dinner – The Secret to Waking Up Fresh

If you struggle to wake up early, your diet might be the culprit.

💡 **Here's the Science:**

- ⇒ 🎯 A heavy, late-night dinner means your body stays busy digesting instead of resting.
- ⇒ 😫 When the morning alarm rings, you feel exhausted instead of refreshed.

Fix It with These Simple Rules:

- ⇒ **Eat before 7 PM** (or at least 3 hours before bedtime).
- ⇒ **Choose light and easily digestible food.**
- ⇒ **Follow Ayurvedic Wisdom:** "Heavy dinners = lazy mornings."

Want to jump out of bed full of energy? Eat early, eat light.

3. Getting Enough Sleep – Quality Over Quantity

Sleep is a superpower—but only if you control it instead of letting it control you!

💡 **The Truth About Sleep:**

- ⇒ Everyone's sleep needs are different:
- ⇒ Some people thrive on just 4-5 hours (think of CEOs and world leaders).
- ⇒ Others need 6-7 hours to function at peak performance.
- ⇒ More than 7 hours? You're probably wasting time and reducing productivity.

🚀 **Finding Your Ideal Sleep Duration:**

To achieve maximum efficiency, find your sweet spot:

⇒ **Experiment for a week** – Sleep different durations and track when you feel most energized.

⇒ **Stick to a fixed sleep schedule** – No excuses, no "just 10 more minutes."

⇒ **Avoid oversleeping** – Too much sleep can leave you feeling sluggish rather than refreshed.

⚖ The Ayurvedic Approach to Sleep:

According to Ayurveda, the quality of rest depends on when you sleep:

⇒ 🕐 9 PM – 12 AM → 1 hour of sleep = 2 hours of rest (deep, rejuvenating sleep)

⇒ 🕐 12 AM – 3 AM → 1 hour of sleep = 1 hour of rest

⇒ 🕐 3 AM – 6 AM → 1 hour of sleep = 0.5 hours of rest (light, less effective sleep)

🌿 The Key Insight:

Sleeping early (before 10 PM) gives double the rest compared to sleeping late. If you sleep at 9 PM to 3AM, six hours feel like nine! This is why Vedic wisdom emphasizes early sleep and waking up before sunrise for peak mental clarity and energy.

💎 Real-Life Examples: How Sleep Impacts Success:

1. Narendra Modi – Thrives on 4-5 hours of sleep!

⇒ His strict sleep schedule helps him run a nation without burnout.

⇒ **Lesson:** Consistency beats duration. Quality sleep > Quantity.

2. Elon Musk – From sleep deprivation to balance.

⇒ The Tesla and SpaceX CEO learned that structured sleep of around 6 hours produces the best output.

⇒ Lesson: Find your optimal sleep time and stick to it!

3. Kobe Bryant – The Mamba Mentality

⇒ The legendary basketball player woke up at 4 AM daily to train while others slept.

⇒ **Lesson:** Sleep enough to perform at your best—but don't oversleep and waste valuable hours.

⌛ **Success is About Balance: Master Your Sleep, Master Your Life!**

⇒ 💤 Too little sleep leads to brain fog, lack of focus, and burnout.

⇒ 😴 Too much sleep means lost hours, regrets, and wasted potential.

⇒ The key? ☑ Follow Ayurveda's wisdom, wake up early, and unlock your peak performance!

Final Thoughts

Your daily habits are the building blocks of success—they shape your mindset, discipline, and ultimately, your results. With these three key habits, you gain the power to become the Avenger of your journey, overcoming challenges and transforming your life.

📌 **The Formula for Success:**

⇒ **Start Small:** Tiny improvements compound into massive success.

⇒ **Stay Consistent:** Discipline is more powerful than fleeting motivation.

⇒ **Eliminate Distractions:** Focus is your superpower.

⇒ **Trust the Process:** Growth takes time, but persistence always pays off.

Remember, extraordinary success comes from ordinary efforts done daily. Embrace these habits and become the Avenger of your journey—empowered, unstoppable, and ready to conquer every challenge.

CHAPTER 6

CONQUER YOUR CLASSROOM: THE ART OF ACTIVE LEARNING FOR SUCCESS

Mastering classroom learning is the key to success. Before every lecture, take a moment to program your mind for success. Close your eyes and repeat:

"I am focused. I am focused. I am focused. I listen actively, understand thoroughly, and make the best notes."

This simple affirmation trains your brain to absorb knowledge efficiently. You are not just a passive listener—you are an active learner.

The Two-Person Rule: Transform the Way You Learn

During the lecture, imagine that only two people exist in the classroom—you and your teacher.

⇒ Assume the teacher is speaking directly to you and respond accordingly.

⇒ Nod when they explain, react when they ask questions, and stay engaged.

⇒ Avoid distractions like chatting with friends or using your phone.

The more involved you are in class, the less time you need to struggle during self-study. Many students hesitate to ask questions because they worry about what others will think. But true learners focus on understanding, not on others' opinions. Your goal is success, not seeking approval.

"सबसे बड़ा रोग, क्या कहेंगे लोग।" (The biggest disease is, "What will people say?")

Pre-Lecture Preparation: Make Your Classroom Lectures More Interesting

To boost your engagement, consider preparing for your lectures in advance.

⇒ **Preview the Material:**

⇒ Study the chapter or watch a one-shot overview of the topic before heading to class the next day.

⇒ **Benefits:**

⇒ This simple step helps you build context and connect new information with what you already know, making the lecture more interesting and easier to follow.

Get the Maximum Out of Every Lecture

⇒ **Invest Wisely:**

⇒ You've invested your time and your parents' hard-earned money in coaching, so make every session count.

⇒ **Immediate Doubt Clearing:**

⇒ Ask questions immediately instead of postponing them.

⇒ **Structured Note-Taking:**

⇒ Take clear and well-organized notes for easy revision.

⇒ **Full Engagement:**

⇒ Being physically present in class is not enough—your mind should be fully engaged. A distracted mind in class means extra effort later when studying on your own.

⇒ **Aim for 60-70% Study in Class:**

⇒ Active participation during lectures helps you cover most of your study material. Understanding concepts in class reduces the time needed for revision and problem-solving later, leading to better retention and effortless recall during exams.

Final Thought: Make Every Lecture Count

Every class is an opportunity to learn, grow, and get closer to your goals. Treat each lecture as a personal session where the teacher is explaining just to you. The more focused and prepared you are, the easier your self-study will become. Stay committed, avoid distractions, and use your class time wisely. By mastering this habit, you set yourself up for academic success effortlessly.

CHAPTER 7

MASTERING THE SKILL OF MAKING EFFECTIVE NOTES IN CLASS

Class notes are a powerful tool for exam preparation. They capture your teacher's explanations, shortcuts, and tricks—things that books may not always provide. Making effective notes the right way can improve retention and make revision faster.

Why Are Class Notes Important?

⇒ Saves time—revising from notes is much faster than rereading books.

⇒ Captures the teacher's insights and explanations beyond the textbook.

⇒ Improves memory retention—writing in your own handwriting strengthens recall.

⇒ A combination of NCERT and class notes can cover up to 80% of JEE/NEET preparation.

How to Make Smart Notes in Class?

1. Write Everything the Teacher Writes on the Board

⇒ Keep notes structured with clear headings and subheadings.

⇒ Leave space for additional points and examples.

2. Capture the Teacher's Verbal Explanations and Examples

⇒ Teachers often share real-life analogies, shortcuts, and tricks that aren't in books—note them down.

⇒ These extra points can make difficult topics easier to understand.

3. Use Different Colors for Better Retention

⇒ Main concepts and definitions should be in one color.

⇒ Important facts, dates, and exceptions should be highlighted separately.

⇒ Formulas and reactions should stand out to make them easy to locate.

⇒ Shortcuts and tricks should be marked clearly for quick reference.

4. Include Diagrams, Flowcharts, and Mind Maps

⇒ For chemistry and biology, use diagrams and reaction flowcharts.

⇒ For physics and maths, highlight formulas, derivation steps, and key problem-solving strategies.

5. Write in Your Own Language

⇒ Use the language you are most comfortable with, whether English, Hindi, or your mother tongue.

⇒ The goal is better understanding, not complicated language.

How to Use Class Notes Effectively?

⇒ **Revise the Same Day** – Reviewing notes within 24 hours improves memory. Highlight key points for faster revision later.

⇒ **Make Short Revision Notes** – After completing a chapter, summarize it in 1-2 pages focusing on formulas, reactions, and difficult concepts.

⇒ **Match Notes with NCERT** – Cross-check with NCERT after making notes to ensure no important points are missing. Add extra details if needed.

⇒ **Use Notes for Last-Minute Revision** – Before exams, avoid big books and rely on your notes for quick revision. Underline weak areas and focus on them in the final days.

Coaching Notes vs. Books – What Matters More?

Your coaching notes are more valuable than bulky textbooks. Books are useful for practice, but notes are your personal key to revision and understanding.

    ⇒ First, master NCERT and your class notes.

    ⇒ Then, use reference books for extra practice.

By following this note-making strategy, you will save time, improve retention, and boost confidence in your exam preparation.

CHAPTER 8

THE RIGHT WAY OF SELF-STUDY – YOUR MASTER KEY TO ALL INDIA RANKS

Self-study is the most crucial factor in cracking JEE/NEET. Even the best coaching and teachers can only guide you—the real progress happens when you sit down and study on your own. But are you studying the right way? Here's how to maximize your efficiency and retention with proven strategies.

Strategy 1: The APE Model

Many students waste time treating all topics equally. Smart students focus on high-weightage areas first. The APE model helps you study effectively:

A – Analysis:

⇒ Review the last 10 years' JEE/NEET papers.

⇒ Identify the high-weightage topics from each chapter.

P – Planning:

⇒ Categorize topics into three sections:

⇒ **High Weightage:** Topics that account for 80% of questions in past papers.

⇒ **Base Topics:** Foundational concepts that support high-weightage areas.

⇒ **Others:** Remaining topics.

⇒ Focus more on the first two categories since time is limited.

⇒ Create a daily, weekly, and monthly study schedule with clear targets.

E – Execution:

⇒ Stick to your plan with consistency.

⇒ Execute your plan with determination.

⇒ Avoid distractions and track your progress daily.

Remember, the difference between toppers and average students is in the execution!

Strategy 2: The Sandwich Model

Divide your daily self-study into three parts for maximum retention:

Part 1 – Theory:

⇒ Revise what was taught in class the same day.

⇒ Read your notes as soon as you get home to boost memory retention.

⇒ Quickly review the chapter's key points to reinforce learning.

Part 2 – MCQ Solving:

⇒ Solve MCQs based on the theory you studied.

⇒ As you solve, note any new points or shortcuts in the space you've left in your notes.

⇒ Maintain an "Error Notebook" to record mistakes and revisit them weekly.

Part 3 – Quick Revision:

⇒ Regularly revisit past chapters, focusing on concepts, formulas, reactions, and key facts.

⇒ Use flashcards, mind maps, and one-page summaries for faster recall.

⇒ Ideal revision times are before bed or immediately after waking up.

Strategy 3: Consistency is Key

⇒ Set a fixed study schedule: aim for a minimum of 6 hours a day and gradually increase by 30 minutes until you reach at least 8 hours.

⇒ Consistency in your study hours builds a strong foundation and eliminates the need for constant adjustments based on mood.

Final Best Practice

Before sleeping, take a few minutes to revise important formulas, concepts, and notes. This nightly review improves long-term retention and deep learning.

By following these strategies, your self-study will become more structured, efficient, and results-driven. Stay consistent, and success will follow!

CHAPTER 9

POWERFUL REVISION STRATEGIES

Revision is the key to long-term success. If you're not in touch with the material, it will gradually fade from your memory. In this chapter, I'll share powerful techniques to help you quickly review formulas, facts, concepts, and reactions. Focus on the high-weightage content first, and cover the rest if time permits. Let's explore these revision strategies to transform you into the superman of your journey.

Audio Learning Strategy – Learn Without Sitting Down to Study

Want to outperform your peers without adding extra study hours? The secret is to use your "dead time" wisely. Successful students not only study harder—they study smarter. With audio learning, you can master concepts without sitting down for traditional study sessions.

⇒ **Record Key Content:**

⇒ Record important concepts, formulas, definitions, and reactions in your own voice. Save these recordings on your phone.

⇒ **Listen During Routine Activities:**

⇒ While brushing, bathing, or even during short breaks

⇒ During travel (if you're not driving)

⇒ At breakfast, lunch, or dinner

⇒ While exercising or during other daily activities

⇒ You can even play them on loudspeakers during your morning routine—just like listening to your favorite songs. Use headphones when you're in public.

⇒ **Reinforce Learning:**

⇒ Repeat the formulas aloud as you listen. This helps your brain retain the information faster.

⇒ **Consistency Is Key:**

⇒ Listen to the same audio for 21 days before switching to a new topic. To speed up learning, you can increase playback speed to 1.25x or 1.5x.

Some might think, "Have you gone mad? Isn't that too much?" I believe that extra effort is natural for those who love learning. True success comes to those who focus on effort consistently—even if it means being a little "mad" about learning. Keep this strategy as your secret weapon; let it fuel your success.

Visual Learning Strategy – Learn Without Really Trying

Your surroundings can be a powerful revision tool if used correctly.

⇒ **Display Key Information:**

⇒ Print out formula charts and place them where you often look.

⇒ Stick formulas on your bathroom mirror to review while brushing.

⇒ Place key concepts on your wardrobe door for a quick glance as you dress.

⇒ Keep important information on your study table for easy reference.

By seeing the same concepts daily, your brain absorbs the information passively, reinforcing retention without extra effort.

The 3-Wall Revision Technique

Many students struggle with revision, often forgetting concepts or feeling overwhelmed before exams. This technique makes revision structured and effortless.

1. **Dedicate Three Walls in Your Room:**

⇒ One wall for physics

⇒ One wall for chemistry

⇒ One wall for maths (or biology)

2. **Create and Display Summaries:**

3. After completing each chapter, summarize the key points on charts. Use different colors to categorize:

⇒ Concepts

⇒ Facts

⇒ Formulas

⇒ Reactions

⇒ Stick these charts on the respective subject wall. Glancing at them daily will reinforce your learning.

4. **Structured Daily Revision:**

5. When the content grows too much to review every day, divide the revision:

⇒ **Monday:** Revise all physics concepts.

⇒ **Tuesday:** Go through chemistry reactions and formulas.

⇒ **Wednesday:** Review maths formulas and zoology facts.

⇒ **Thursday:** Focus on additional chemistry facts.

⇒ **Friday:** Recall physics formulas and key points.

⇒ **Saturday:** Study maths theorems and botany facts.

⇒ **Sunday:** Revise weak areas across all subjects.

Stick to this strategy—daily revision using the 3-wall technique will set you on the path to becoming AIR 1. Come on, you can do it!

Final Results

By applying these revision strategies, you'll experience:

> ⇒ **No Last-Minute Exam Stress:** Confidence builds when you know you've reviewed regularly.

> ⇒ **Faster Recall of Concepts:** Structured revision makes information retrieval quick and easy.

> ⇒ **Better Long-Term Retention:** Consistent reinforcement cements learning.

> ⇒ **Higher Efficiency:** You maximize learning during dead time without extra study hours.

Using dead time wisely, leveraging visual learning techniques, and following a structured revision plan will help you master subjects effortlessly. Start applying these strategies today and take your learning to the next level!

CHAPTER 10

NCERT – YOUR ULTIMATE WEAPON FOR SUCCESS

NCERT: The Golden Key to Success in JEE & NEET

A common mistake many students make is undervaluing NCERT and chasing big, bulky books too soon. Let this be crystal clear:

"NCERT is not just a book—it's your foundation, your roadmap, and your ticket to success in national exams!"

Your Study Priority (In the Right Order!)

⇒ **Step 1: Master NCERT (100%)**

    ⇒ Read every line of NCERT carefully—many direct questions come from it.

    ⇒ Solve all intext & exercise questions, underlining important points.

    ⇒ For Biology & Chemistry, memorize NCERT diagrams and tables—they are GOLD!

⇒ **Step 2: Class Notes – Your Personal Cheat Code!**

    ⇒ Your teachers already know what's most important—trust their notes.

    ⇒ Organize notes properly (we'll discuss the best note-making strategies later).

    ⇒ Revise handwritten notes regularly to strengthen concepts.

⇒ **Step 3: Reference Books (Choose Wisely!)**

    ⇒ Consult your teachers to pick 2-3 books.

⇒ Use them only after mastering NCERT—they are for additional practice.

The Deadly Trap: Ignoring NCERT & Chasing Big Books!

Many students fall into the "big book syndrome," thinking:

⇒ "NCERT is too basic. I'll focus on tougher books."

⇒ "Toppers solve hundreds of reference book questions, so I should too!"

⇒ "I'll do NCERT later. Let me first solve advanced problems."

Result? They struggle with basics, get stuck in exams, and regret later!

Smart Strategy = NCERT First, Then Reference Books!

Pro Tips for NCERT Mastery

1. Read each chapter 3 times:

⇒ 1st for understanding

⇒ 2nd for note-making

⇒ 3rd for retention

2. Highlight tricky concepts and revise them regularly.

3. Make NCERT-based short notes & flashcards for quick revision.

4. Solve Previous Year Questions (PYQs) that are directly based on NCERT—this will boost confidence.

Final Words

"NCERT is like a skeleton—without it, your preparation has no structure. Reference books are like muscles—they add strength, but only if the skeleton is strong!"

So, first **BUILD the skeleton, then ADD strength!**

CHAPTER 11

DOUBTS ARE DEMONS – KILL THEM BEFORE THEY KILL YOU

Doubts are like termites—if not cleared in time, they slowly eat away at your confidence and interest in the subject. In subjects like Physics, Chemistry, Maths, and Biology, even a small doubt today can become a huge roadblock later. Here's how to conquer doubts like a topper with a simple 3-step formula.

3-Step Formula to Conquer Doubts

1. Never Sleep with a Doubt

⇒ **Immediate Action:**

⇒ The moment a doubt arises, write it down immediately.

⇒ Set a specific time every day for clearing doubts—after class, during short breaks, or in dedicated doubt sessions.

2. Ask the Right People – The Best Doubt-Solving Order

⇒ **Step 1: Teachers & Coaching Faculty**

⇒ Your teachers understand your learning style and can offer personalized guidance. Ensure your coaching environment encourages questions.

⇒ **Step 2: Friends Who Are Ahead of You**

⇒ Peer learning can be very effective. A friend who grasps a concept better can explain it in a way that resonates with you.

⇒ **Step 3: Textbooks & Reference Books**

⇒ If your teacher or friends are unavailable, refer to NCERT and other standard reference books (e.g., HC Verma, OP Tandon, MS Chauhan, etc.).

⇒ **Important Note on Online Platforms:**

⇒ Although online platforms like Google, YouTube, or even ChatGPT can sometimes provide quick help, I do not recommend relying on them for doubt clearing. They can often offer incorrect answers and should be used only in worst-case scenarios when face-to-face guidance isn't available. The best approach is to ask live, directly from someone knowledgeable.

3. Maintain a 'Doubt Diary'

⇒ **Keep Track:**

⇒ Dedicate a notebook exclusively for your doubts.

⇒ After getting an answer, write a summary of the solution in your own words.

⇒ **Review Regularly:**

⇒ Review old doubts every weekend to reinforce learning and ensure long-term retention.

Warning: Don't Let Doubts Become Backlogs!

If you keep postponing clearing your doubts, a small question may snowball into a major gap in your understanding. One small doubt can lead to a skipped concept, which in turn can make an entire chapter difficult and increase exam pressure. Remember:

"Ignoring a doubt is like ignoring a crack in a dam—it will burst sooner or later!"

CHAPTER 12

3 GAME CHANGERS THAT WILL SET YOU APART FROM OTHERS

Simple yet most powerful techniques that most successful people believe and follow that i learnt from my Gurus and coaches which changed my life and mindset.Now i m going to share you. this will transform you from ordinary to extraordinary personality.

1. Affirmations

Your **mindset** is the foundation of your success. Preparing for **JEE/NEET** is not just about studying hard—it's about **thinking like a topper.** The way you **talk to yourself** and the way you **see your progress** determines whether you will succeed or struggle.

Great achievers don't just have talent; they have a **strong mindset** built on **affirmations and gratitude.** Let's learn how to develop the same mindset!

Programming Your Mind for Success with Affirmations

⇒ Affirmations are **positive statements** that help rewire your brain for **confidence and focus.**

⇒ What you tell yourself daily becomes your **belief system**—so why not program your mind for **success?**

⇒ **Example: Virat Kohli** visualized himself as a **world-class cricketer** before achieving success. His **belief in himself** turned into reality.

Sample Affirmations for you

> ⇒ *I am focused and capable; I can overcome any challenge.*

> ⇒ *Every day, I grow smarter and more confident in my abilities.*

> ⇒ *I master concepts quickly and apply them with ease.*

> ⇒ *I embrace challenges as opportunities to learn and improve.*

> ⇒ *I am calm, composed, and ready for every exam.*

> ⇒ *My hard work and consistency pave the way for my success.*

> ⇒ *I trust my intuition and knowledge to guide me through difficult problems.*

> ⇒ *I am determined to achieve my dreams and create a bright future.*

> ⇒ *I absorb and retain information effortlessly.*

> ⇒ *Every step I take brings me closer to my goal of success in JEE/NEET.*

How to Practice Affirmations Effectively?

> ⇒ Say them with **confidence & energy** every morning.

> ⇒ Repeat at least **7 times** aloud or write 7 times on a notebook with faith

> ⇒ Believe in what you are saying—your mind will **start working** toward making it true!

Why Do Affirmations Work?

> ⇒ Your **brain adapts** to the identity you reinforce.

> ⇒ The more you say it, the more you **think, act, and feel** like a **top ranker.**

> ⇒ You naturally become **disciplined, focused, and resistant to distractions.**

2. Gratitude

"If you are not grateful, you are great fool"

> **– HH Radhanath Swami**

Shifting to a Positive Mindset with Gratitude

⇒ **A grateful mind** is a **powerful mind.** Instead of stressing over what you don't have, focus on what you **already have.**

⇒ Gratitude removes **negativity**, increases **motivation**, and makes you feel **stronger** even in tough times.

⇒ It helps in release of dopamine hormones required for our frontal lobes to work effectively

Example:

⇒ **Oprah Winfrey**, one of the most successful media personalities, credits much of her success to her **daily gratitude journaling.** She once said:

⇒ *"If you focus on what you don't have, you will never have enough. If you focus on what you have, you will always have more."*

How to Practice Gratitude Daily?

⇒ Every night, write down **3 things you are grateful for.**

⇒ **It could be as simple as your younger sister gave you a glass of water as soon as you reached home in sunny day.**

Here are some examples of gratitude journal entries for you to understand how to write

⇒ **March 1, 2025**

⇒ *Today, I'm really grateful to God for giving me the strength to keep pushing through my studies, even when things felt overwhelming. I felt a sense of calm during my exam prep, and I know His guidance is with me.*

$\Rightarrow$ **March 2, 2025**

$\Rightarrow$ *I'm thankful for my mom today. Her warm hug and encouraging words this morning made me believe I can tackle any challenge. I appreciate how she always makes time to listen, even on my busiest days.*

$\Rightarrow$ **March 3, 2025**

$\Rightarrow$ *I want to thank my dad for his constant support. When I was worried about my project, he sat with me and helped me sort through my ideas. I'm grateful for his practical advice and the way he cheers me on every day.*

$\Rightarrow$ **March 4, 2025**

$\Rightarrow$ *Today, I felt really lucky for my teacher, Mrs. Sharma, who took extra time after class to explain a tricky concept. Her patience and passion for teaching inspire me to do my best.*

$\Rightarrow$ **March 5, 2025**

$\Rightarrow$ *I'm grateful for my friends. Whether we're laughing during lunch or supporting each other through tough homework sessions, they make every day more fun and less stressful. I appreciate our late-night study group too!*

$\Rightarrow$ **March 6, 2025**

$\Rightarrow$ *I spent some time outside today and felt a deep connection with nature. The fresh air and the sound of birds chirping gave me a much-needed break from screen time. I'm thankful for the little moments of peace that nature brings.*

$\Rightarrow$ **March 7, 2025**

$\Rightarrow$ *Even my challenges have something to teach me. I'm grateful for that classmate who always debates with me—even when we don't see eye to eye. Their challenge pushes me to think harder and grow stronger.*

3. Mantra Meditation

Mantra meditation is a practice that has helped me find inner calm and sharpen my focus on my work. It is essential to increase your focus on your study and have mental stability. Mantra is a sanskrit word which means "one that delivers the mind". By repeating a mantra you quiet the mind and create space for your true potential to emerge.

How to Practice Mantra Meditation

⇒ **Choose Your Mantra:**

⇒ You can use the mantra "Hare Krishna Hare Krishna Krishna Krishna Hare Hare, Hare Rama Hare Rama Rama Rama Hare Hare." If you're Muslim, Christian, or follow another faith, feel free to chant your religious mantra. Choose a mantra that resonates with you.

⇒ **Find a Quiet Space:**

⇒ Sit comfortably in a quiet spot where you won't be disturbed. Close your eyes and take a few deep, calm breaths.

⇒ **Repeat the Mantra:**

⇒ Slowly and steadily, repeat your mantra aloud. Let the sound vibration of the mantra anter your ears and make sure your mind is focused completely.

⇒ **Focus on Your Breath:**

⇒ Combine your mantra with deep, rhythmic breathing. Inhale deeply and, as you exhale, let your mantra flow with your breath.

⇒ **Regular Practice:**

⇒ Aim for at least 5–10 minutes of mantra meditation every day. Over time, gradually extend the duration as you grow more comfortable.

Benefits of Mantra Meditation

⇒ **Reduces Stress:** It lowers anxiety and calms exam-related stress.

⇒ **Improves Concentration:** Regular practice enhances your focus during study sessions.

⇒ **Boosts Mental Clarity:** Clears mental clutter, making it easier to process and retain information.

⇒ **Fosters Inner Peace:** Cultivates a sense of calm and resilience that carries over into every area of your life.

Embrace mantra meditation as a daily ritual, and let your chosen mantra—whether it's "Hare Krishna..." or your own sacred chant—guide you to a state of focused calm. This practice is one of the three game changers that will set you apart from others on your journey to success.

Final Thought: The Mindset of a Winner

Imagine yourself already achieving your dreams. Believe in your potential and take action every day. A positive mind leads to positive actions, and positive actions lead to great success. Embrace affirmations, practice gratitude, and make mantra meditation a daily ritual. Master these three game changers, and no one can stop you from becoming an All India Ranker!

Start today—and watch your mindset transform your future!

CHAPTER 13

THE POWER OF FOCUS – GUARD YOUR INPUTS FOR GUARANTEED SUCCESS

If you truly want to secure an All India Rank, there's one golden rule you must follow:

Avoid distractions at all costs

Most students don't fail because they lack intelligence or effort; they fail because they lose focus. The greatest enemy of your success isn't difficulty—it's distraction.

Why Do Students Lose Focus?

Ever wondered why you sometimes feel restless, demotivated, or unable to concentrate? It comes down to one simple thing—the **inputs** you allow into your mind through your eyes and ears.

Your mind works like a computer:

Wrong inputs → Wrong outputs

Right inputs → Powerful focus and energy

If you constantly fill your mind with negativity and distractions, your brain will struggle to concentrate on studying effectively.

Eliminate These Focus Killers

1. Internet Overload

⇒ Random browsing, unnecessary YouTube videos, and jumping between study sources destroy deep concentration.

⇒ **Smart Tip:** Use parental control apps or site blockers to keep yourself focused.

2. Social Media Trap

⇒ Instagram, Snapchat, Facebook, and WhatsApp steal hours without you realizing it.

⇒ **Smart Tip:** Temporarily delete or disable these apps during your preparation. Trust me, you're not missing anything truly valuable.

3. Toxic Friend Circle

⇒ Not all friends help you succeed. Friends who gossip or spread negativity harm your mindset and distract you even when you're alone.

⇒ **Smart Tip:** Choose friends who motivate, encourage, and push you closer to your dreams.

4. Negative Relatives & Energy Drainers

⇒ Some people might tell you, "JEE/NEET is too tough," "What if you fail?" or "It's not your cup of tea."

⇒ **Smart Tip:** Ignore these negative voices. Surround yourself only with people who uplift and believe in your abilities.

5. TV, OTT & Entertainment Addiction

⇒ Binge-watching TV, movies, or cricket matches might seem relaxing but steals precious preparation time.

⇒ **Smart Tip:** Avoid entertainment completely during these two critical years. If you must, set strict weekly study targets and reward yourself with limited viewing (max 1 hour per week).

The 2-Year Discipline Rule

If you're fully serious about your success, make this clear decision today:

"I will eliminate distractions for two years to achieve lifetime success."

Ask yourself honestly:

⇒ What's more important to me—temporary entertainment or lasting success?

⇒ Do I prefer short-term pleasure or long-term achievement?

Your answer defines your future.

The Guaranteed Success Formula

Control Your Inputs → Sharpen Your Focus → Achieve Guaranteed Success

Final Words: Become a Warrior of Focus!

⇒ Guard your mind like a fortress.

⇒ Filter carefully everything that enters through your eyes and ears.

⇒ Choose your friends and environment wisely.

⇒ Stay disciplined. Stay focused. Become unstoppable.

The power of your focus is the power of your success—**Guard it fiercely!**

CHAPTER 14

FROM LOW SCORES TO CHAMPIONS – THE MINDSET OF TRUE ACHIEVERS

Every topper, every achiever, and every game-changer in history has faced failure, self-doubt, and defeat. But what sets them apart?

⇒ They did not let failure define them—they used it as fuel to rise even higher.

⇒ Most students get demotivated by low scores and start believing they aren't "smart enough" or "capable enough."

⇒ Even parents sometimes assume that their child is not meant for big things.

⇒ But here's the truth: **Your score is not YOU.** It's just a number that reflects where you stand today, not where you will be tomorrow.

If you feel disheartened by a bad test, ask yourself:

⇒ Am I going to let this one moment decide my future?

⇒ Or am I going to fight back harder, learn from my mistakes, and turn things around?

Real-Life Proof: Failures Don't Define You

1. Elon Musk – From Job Rejection to World-Changing Success

⇒ Before Elon Musk became famous for founding companies like Tesla and SpaceX, he faced big setbacks. In his early career, he was rejected when he applied for a job at Netscape, a leading tech company at the time. Later, Musk started PayPal, but was fired from his own company by the people working with him. Imagine how tough it must have felt to be turned down for a job and then removed from your own company! Yet Musk didn't lose heart. Instead, he learned from these experiences, kept going, and eventually founded Tesla and SpaceX. Today, he's considered one of the greatest innovators of our time.

⇒ **Lesson:**

⇒ *Every rejection can push you toward bigger and better things.*

2. Michael Jordan – Rejected from His School Team to NBA Legend

⇒ Michael Jordan, known today as one of the greatest basketball players ever, faced serious disappointment as a teenager. When he was in high school, he was dropped from his school basketball team. The coach thought he wasn't good enough. Instead of feeling sorry for himself, Jordan decided to practice harder. He spent hours every day practicing his basketball skills. Within a year, his efforts paid off—he not only made it back onto the team but became their star player. Jordan later won six NBA championships, inspiring millions around the world.

⇒ **Lesson:**

⇒ *When someone doubts you, let it motivate you to prove them wrong.*

3. Virat Kohli – From Struggles to Cricket Superstar

⇒ Virat Kohli, one of India's greatest cricketers, faced several setbacks early in his career. As a young player, he often performed poorly in important matches and faced harsh criticism. Many people wondered if he had what it took to succeed. Instead of letting this discourage him, Kohli worked even harder, training intensely and improving his fitness. With determination and practice, he grew from a struggling young player into one of the world's best cricketers and a successful team captain.

⇒ **Lesson:**

⇒ *Your failures today don't define your future. Keep working, and you will succeed.*

The Real Secret to Success

⇒ **Failures Are Not the End—They Are Stepping Stones!**

    ⇒ Champions don't let failures break them. They use failures to build themselves.

    ⇒ Every time you fall, rise stronger. Learn from it. Improve.

⇒ **As Lord Krishna said in the Bhagavad Gita:**

⇒ *"You have the right to perform your duty, but you are not entitled to the fruits of your actions."*

    ⇒ Stop stressing about results. Focus on effort, growth, and learning.

The Champion Mindset – Here's What You Must Do!

⇒ **See Failure as Feedback, Not as a Judgment**

    ⇒ Low scores don't mean you're a failure—they show you where to improve.

⇒ **Identify Mistakes, Track Them, Fix Them!**

    ⇒ Keep a **Mistake Journal** where you write down errors and strategies to fix them.

⇒ **Train Like a Warrior – Consistency Wins Battles**

    ⇒ One bad test doesn't decide your future. But quitting does.

Your Time Will Come – Make It Happen!

⇒ This is **YOUR** journey, **YOUR** dream, **YOUR** future.

⇒ Are you ready to fight for it? To rise above setbacks? To prove yourself?

If you truly embrace this mindset, **nothing can stop you.**

And one day, when you achieve your goal, you will become an inspiration for others—just like the legends before you!

CHAPTER 15

THE POWER OF RESPECT – THE KEY TO SUCCESS

As a student, I always respected all my teachers deeply—no matter their teaching style or how they treated me. This quality was a precious gift from my mother, who taught me to honor everyone older than me. And guess what? That simple act of respect changed my life completely.

Because I showed genuine respect, my teachers went beyond just teaching me subjects—they shared invaluable life lessons. Some taught wisdom from the Bhagavad Gita, others from the Bible, and many from their personal experiences. At that time, I didn't fully understand why they cared for me so deeply, almost like their own child. Now, looking back, I realize it was exactly the support and love I needed. Maybe it was God's way of guiding me through them.

This respect wasn't just limited to my teachers. To this day, I've never raised my voice against my parents—even though my father and I often held opposite views. No matter how strongly we disagreed, I always knew deep inside that his intentions were pure and he wanted the very best for me.

Sure, maybe he didn't always find the perfect words to guide me, but his heart was always in the right place. Every word he spoke and every decision he made was rooted in concern and love. Understanding this, I never felt the need to argue. Instead, I developed patience, gratitude, and the wisdom to listen.

However, today when I see students disrespecting their teachers—chatting during class, mocking them, or complaining about their parents—it hurts. More importantly, it worries me deeply because many students don't realize how much this behavior negatively affects their lives.

Discipline isn't about restrictions. It's about shaping yourself into a strong, successful, and respected individual. And discipline begins with respect.

Here are three powerful forms of respect that can change your life:

1. Respecting Teachers – Unlocking Knowledge

Knowledge flows just like water—from higher to lower levels. When we respect our teachers, we naturally absorb their knowledge better and faster. The moment we stop valuing them, we create a barrier between ourselves and true learning.

Have you ever noticed it's tough to focus on a subject if you dislike your teacher? Ever wondered why some students excel with the same teacher, while others struggle? It's not just about talent—it's about attitude. Your attitude decides your altitude. Respect your teachers, and learning becomes effortless.

2. Respecting Parents – Your Greatest Well-Wishers

We often take our parents for granted. They love us unconditionally, yet we easily get irritated, argue, or ignore their advice. Think for a moment— who else sacrifices sleep, dreams, and comfort just to see you succeed? Only your parents.

But how do most students react?

⟹ "Mom, stop nagging!"

⟹ "Dad, you just don't understand!"

Behind their every word is pure love and deep concern. No teacher, friend, or relative wants your success more genuinely than your parents do. Discipline means controlling your emotions and responding with gratitude instead of irritation. Next time, before raising your voice, ask yourself:

⟹ Would I speak this way to my best friend?

⟹ What if this was the last time I heard their advice?

When you start respecting your parents, life starts honoring you.

3. Respecting the Opposite Sex – Protect Your Future

Teenage years bring powerful distractions—emotions, hormones, and societal pressures disguised as "love" and "fun." Here's the truth: most teenage relationships don't last, but their impact does:

- ⇒ Lost focus
- ⇒ Broken hearts
- ⇒ Regrets
- ⇒ Damaged reputations

Prevention is always better than cure. Respecting the opposite gender doesn't mean avoiding them—it means maintaining dignity and clarity of purpose. Think of your goal as a train journey to success; distractions are unnecessary stops. If you keep getting off at every stop, you'll never reach your destination. Stay on track—your time will come. Build your future first.

The Power of Being a True Disciple

The word "disciple" comes from "discipline." Discipline is about self-respect, self-control, and self-mastery.

Great learners in history—like Arjuna who learned from Krishna, Chandragupta who learned from Chanakya, or even modern achievers—all shared one common trait: deep respect for their teachers, parents, and principles.

So, ask yourself today:

- ⇒ Do I truly respect my teachers, or just tolerate them?
- ⇒ Do I see my parents as my greatest support, or do I ignore their wisdom?
- ⇒ Am I protecting my future, or letting temporary distractions steal my focus?

The choice is yours. Respect your teachers, honor your parents, and safeguard your future. When you master respect and discipline, success is inevitable.

CHAPTER 16

CELEBRATE, CORRECT & CONQUER!

There will be days when no one notices your effort. No one will see how hard you studied, how many distractions you fought, or how much you pushed yourself to be better than yesterday. You might have improved by 10 marks, but instead of a "Well done!", all you hear is, "Still not good enough."

It hurts, doesn't it?

But let me tell you something—you don't need anyone's approval to celebrate your progress!

Clap for Yourself First

Success is not about one big moment when the world applauds you. It's built on thousands of small victories that no one sees. And if you don't learn to acknowledge and cherish them, you might lose the motivation to keep going.

⇒ Did you finally understand a tough concept? Reward yourself with a chocolate.

⇒ Studied consistently for a week? Treat yourself to your favorite snack.

⇒ Woke up on time and completed your study goals? Give yourself a little break and enjoy your favorite music.

These little self-rewards remind you that your efforts matter. The day will come when the world will clap for you—but until then, be your own biggest cheerleader!

Be Strong Enough to Correct Yourself

Now, just as success must be celebrated, failures must be owned.

If you don't reach your target because of laziness or distractions, don't make excuses. Instead, discipline yourself.

⇒ Wasted time on social media? Reduce your entertainment time the next day.

⇒ Didn't complete your assignments? Wake up 30 minutes earlier and finish them.

⇒ Skipped an important revision? Cancel your fun outing and make up for it.

Success is not about never failing—it's about correcting yourself every time you slip.

Take Charge of Your Own Life

One day, people will praise your achievements. They will admire your success. But the truth is—they weren't there when you fought your inner battles, stayed up late, and kept going when no one believed in you.

And that's why you must take charge of your own journey.

⇒ Reward yourself when you move forward.

⇒ Discipline yourself when you slip.

⇒ Take responsibility for your own growth.

⇒ Never wait for someone to appreciate you. Never depend on someone to push you. Be your own coach. Be your own hero. Because the ones who learn to manage themselves... become unstoppable!

Now, are you ready to take charge and conquer your life?

CHAPTER 17

THE MINDSET OF CHAMPIONS – THINK LIKE A WINNER

Success isn't only about talent or hard work—it's about your mindset. If success had a formula, it would be 80% mindset and just 20% effort. The difference between an average student and a topper isn't intelligence, but how they think.

Many students fail, not because they lack ability, but because they allow self-doubt, negativity, and distractions to hold them back. Champions, however, train their minds to stay focused, determined, and resilient. To achieve success in JEE, NEET, or any goal you set, start by developing a winning mindset.

Here are key principles that can transform your thinking and make success guaranteed:

1. Break Through Limiting Beliefs

Most failures start in the mind. If you believe you can't do something, you won't even try.

Negative thoughts like "I'm not good at Physics" or "I can't crack JEE/NEET" are not facts—they're just limiting beliefs.

Your brain believes what you repeatedly tell it. Change your thinking:

⇒ "I can master this if I keep trying."

⇒ "I haven't succeeded yet, but I will."

2. Stop Blaming, Mourning, and Complaining (The BMC Trap)

Winners take responsibility; losers blame others.

Complaining about tough exams, poor teaching, or lack of support changes nothing.

Success comes to those who take control, look for solutions, and keep moving forward.

3. See Every Failure as an Opportunity

Every great achiever failed multiple times before succeeding.

⇒ Thomas Edison failed 10,000 times before inventing the light bulb.

Instead of saying, "I failed," say, "I learned."

Treat every mistake as a lesson that moves you closer to success.

4. Surround Yourself with Motivated People

The people you spend your time with shape your mindset.

⇒ Spend time with goal-oriented students who inspire you.

⇒ Avoid distractions, toxic friendships, and negativity.

If you surround yourself with winners, you naturally start thinking and acting like one.

5. Follow Proven Strategies, Not Random Experiments

Many students waste valuable time experimenting with random methods.

⇒ Learn from successful students and toppers.

⇒ Follow study techniques and routines that have proven effective.

Why reinvent the wheel when you can learn from those who have already succeeded?

6. Ignore Demotivators & Negative People

Some people will try to discourage you:

⇒ "JEE/NEET is too hard."

⇒ "Only geniuses succeed."

⇒ "What if you fail?"

Protect your energy—don't let negativity enter your mind. Believe in yourself, even when others doubt you. Your success will be your best answer.

7. Use the CAR Method – Change, Accept, Replace

⇒ **C – Change the Changeable:** Change your useless friends, study methods, and mindset.

⇒ **A – Accept the Unchangeable:** Accept exam patterns, syllabus, or external conditions.

⇒ **R – Reject or Replace the Unacceptable:** Eliminate unproductive routines, distractions, and bad influences.

Master this method, and no obstacle can stop you.

Success Is a Mindset

Champions aren't born—they're made through discipline, perseverance, and attitude.

⇒ Break limiting beliefs.

⇒ Take responsibility.

⇒ Turn problems into opportunities.

⇒ Follow proven paths.

⇒ Reject negativity.

⇒ Practice the CAR method daily.

Final Thought

Your mindset determines your success. Think and act like a winner, and success will surely follow.

Now, ask yourself honestly: Are you ready to think like a champion?

CHAPTER 18

THE POWER OF SPIRITUALITY: THE HIDDEN SECRET OF SUCCESS

💡 *"A positive mind finds opportunity in everything. A negative mind finds fault in everything."*

Your mind is your most powerful weapon in this journey toward success. But have you ever thought about what you are feeding it? Just like the body needs nutritious food, your mind also needs pure, positive, and powerful inputs to function at its best.

Most students believe that success comes only from studying harder. But the truth is, mental stability, focus, and inner strength are equally important. And the greatest source of mental power is **spiritual wisdom.**

The Secret Behind All Great Achievers

⇒ Albert Einstein read the Bhagavad Gita for wisdom.

⇒ Dr. A.P.J. Abdul Kalam started his day with the Bhagavad Gita.

⇒ Steve Jobs was deeply influenced by Hindu philosophy.

⇒ Satya Nadella, the CEO of Microsoft, credits his success to spirituality.

The world's greatest achievers rely on spirituality because it brings **clarity, emotional strength, and unwavering focus**—the three essential ingredients for success.

Why Spirituality is a Game-Changer for Students

1. Inner Peace = Greater Focus

> ⇒ When your mind is filled with anxiety, overthinking, and self-doubt, you cannot concentrate.

> ⇒ Spiritual wisdom helps declutter your thoughts and keeps your mind sharp and stable.

💡 **Try This:** Start your day with even **5-10 minutes of mantra meditation** or **deep breathing**. It will boost your focus and retention power.

2. Bhagavad Gita – The Ultimate Guide for Decision-Making

> ⇒ Life is full of confusions and dilemmas.

> ⇒ Should I study this or that? Should I take a break or push myself? What if I fail?

> ⇒ The **Bhagavad Gita** teaches how to stay strong in tough times, make the right choices, and keep moving forward without fear.

💡 **Try This:** Read just **one verse of Bhagavad Gita daily** and apply it in your life. You'll be amazed at how much mental clarity you gain!

3. Strength to Overcome Failure

> ⇒ Most students break down after getting low scores or facing difficulties.

> ⇒ But spiritual wisdom helps you bounce back stronger.

💡 **Remember Krishna's words in the Bhagavad Gita:**

"You have the right to perform your duty, but you are not entitled to the fruits of your actions."

> ⇒ Success is a **by-product of consistent effort.**

> ⇒ If you focus only on results, you will feel pressure.

⇒ But if you focus on giving your **best effort**, you will eventually succeed.

4. Positive Inputs = Positive Mindset

⇒ Your **thoughts create your reality.**

⇒ If you fill your mind with negativity from **social media, gossip, or self-doubt**, you will feel demotivated.

⇒ But if you feed your mind with **spiritual wisdom**, you will gain confidence, motivation, and inner peace.

💡 **Try This:** Attend at least **one spiritual discourse every week.** It will recharge your mind with positivity.

"Isn't This a Waste of Time? I Could Study More Instead."

Many students think that reading scriptures or attending spiritual discourses takes away valuable study time. But here's the truth:

⇒ **Studying for hours with a distracted mind is ineffective.**

⇒ **Studying with a calm, sharp, and focused mind gives faster results.**

Just like **exercise** improves your physical energy, **spirituality** boosts your **mental energy.**

The top-performing students are not those who study the longest, but those who study with the **sharpest focus.**

How to Apply This in Your Daily Life?

⇒ **Start your day** with a few minutes of **mantra meditation** (e.g., chanting the **Hare Krishna Mahamantra**).

⇒ **Read 1–2 verses** from the Bhagavad Gita every morning.

⇒ **Attend a weekly spiritual discourse** (online or offline).

⇒ **Reflect** on spiritual teachings and apply them in your daily challenges.

Final Words: Your Secret Weapon for Success

While others struggle with **stress, anxiety, and distractions,** you will have an **unshakable mindset**—one that is **calm, focused, and powerful.**

⇒ **A strong mind** leads to **strong actions.**

⇒ **Strong actions** lead to **great results.**

✿ If you take care of your mind, your success is **GUARANTEED.** ✿

CHAPTER 19

WHY EVERYONE NEEDS A COACH?

The Power of a Guru/Mentor in Your Journey

"Even Arjuna needed Krishna as his Guru. Every great achiever had a mentor. You need one too!"

JEE/NEET preparation is not just about studying hard—it's a mental and emotional battle. There will be times when:

⇒ You lose confidence after scoring low in a test.

⇒ You feel confused about what to study and how to proceed.

⇒ You get frustrated with backlogs and difficult topics.

At such times, having the right mentor can make all the difference!

Why Do You Need a Guru/Mentor?

⇒ **They Give You the Right Direction**

  ⇒ A good mentor can filter out distractions and help you focus on what truly matters.

  ⇒ They prevent panic and overthinking, guiding you step by step.

⇒ **They Have Experience & Wisdom**

  ⇒ They have already seen hundreds of students like you—they know what works!

  ⇒ They can tell you the common mistakes to avoid and the fastest way to success.

⇒ **They Keep You Motivated**

 ⇒ When you feel like quitting, your mentor will remind you why you started.

 ⇒ They will boost your confidence and help you get back on track.

⇒ **They Help You Stay Accountable**

 ⇒ When you know your mentor is watching your progress, you automatically become more disciplined.

 ⇒ Regular check-ins with a mentor ensure that you stay consistent.

How to Find the Right Mentor?

Not everyone who gives advice is the right mentor. A true mentor should have these key qualities:

⇒ **Proven Expertise in Your Goal**

 ⇒ Your mentor should have deep knowledge and experience in the field you want to excel in.

 ⇒ Example: If you're preparing for JEE/NEET, a mentor should have either cleared the exam themselves or have years of experience coaching successful students.

⇒ **Strategic Thinking & Problem-Solving Ability**

 ⇒ A great mentor doesn't just teach—they provide study plans, exam strategies, and time-management tips.

 ⇒ Example: If you struggle with organic chemistry, a good mentor will tell you which chapters to master first instead of just telling you to "study harder."

⇒ **Encouraging but Honest Feedback**

 ⇒ The right mentor doesn't just motivate you—they also push you to improve by identifying your weak areas.

⇒ Example: If you fail a mock test, a mentor shouldn't just say "Don't worry." Instead, they should analyze your mistakes and guide you to fix them.

⇒ **Emotional Support & Mental Strength**

⇒ Success is not just about knowledge—it's about mental resilience.

⇒ A good mentor believes in you even when you doubt yourself and helps you stay strong during tough times.

⇒ Example: If you're feeling demotivated, a mentor should remind you why you started and help you regain your focus.

⇒ **Values Discipline & Hard Work**

⇒ A mentor should lead by example and teach you the importance of consistency, discipline, and effort.

⇒ Example: If they guide you to wake up early, follow a study schedule, and avoid distractions, they are shaping your mindset for success.

Where to Find the Right Mentor?

⇒ **Teachers & Coaching Faculty** – They know the syllabus, strategy, and common mistakes students make.

⇒ **A Senior or Past Topper** – Someone who has been through this journey can give practical advice.

⇒ **A Parent or Guide** – Someone who believes in you and keeps you emotionally strong.

⇒ **Spiritual Guru (if you follow one)** – Can give you mental peace and emotional stability.

How to Make the Most of Your Mentor?

Having a great mentor is a privilege, but only if you know how to use their guidance effectively!

⇒ **Ask Questions & Clear Doubts Immediately**

  ⇒ Doubts are like speed breakers—if you don't clear them, they will slow you down.

  ⇒ Never hesitate to ask, no matter how small the doubt seems.

⇒ **Follow Their Advice with Full Faith**

  ⇒ Many students get distracted by too many strategies. If you trust your mentor, follow their plan without doubting it.

  ⇒ Overanalyzing multiple opinions can create confusion and waste valuable time.

⇒ **Stay in Regular Touch**

  ⇒ Don't only approach your mentor when things go wrong—seek guidance regularly.

  ⇒ Consistent communication helps in tracking progress and making necessary improvements.

⇒ **Be Coachable – Keep Ego Aside & Learn**

  ⇒ The best students are those who listen, implement, and adapt.

  ⇒ Be open to constructive criticism and willing to change your approach if needed.

Final Thought: Every Champion Had a Mentor!

⇒ Arjuna had Krishna.

⇒ Chhatrapati Shivaji Maharaj had Samarth Ramdas.

⇒ Alexander had Aristotle.

⇒ APJ Abdul Kalam had Dr. Vikram Sarabhai.

Find your guide, trust them, and move ahead with full confidence!

CHAPTER 20

5 LIFE-CHANGING LESSONS FOR STUDENTS FROM THE BHAGAVAD GITA

The Bhagavad Gita is not just a religious text; it is a spiritual and practical guide for success in any field. It was spoken by Lord Krishna to Arjuna on the battlefield of Kurukshetra—a moment when Arjuna was confused, fearful, and doubting himself.

Just like Arjuna, students today face self-doubt, distractions, fear of failure, and mental pressure. The Gita provides timeless solutions to overcome these struggles and achieve success.

Here are five powerful lessons from the Bhagavad Gita As It Is that can help you stay focused, fearless, and determined on your academic journey.

Lesson 1: Focus on Your Duty, Not the Results

कर्मण्येवाधिकारस्ते मा फलेषु कदाचन।

मा कर्मफलहेतुर्भूर्मा ते सङ्गोऽस्त्वकर्मणि॥

"You have a right to perform your prescribed duties, but you are not entitled to the fruits of action. Never consider yourself the cause of the results of your activities, nor be attached to inaction." (Bhagavad Gita 2.47)

- ⇒ Many students worry too much about marks, ranks, and competition. This creates stress and reduces efficiency.

- ⇒ Krishna's advice: Focus on the process, not the outcome.

- ⇒ If you put in 100% honest effort, the results will take care of themselves.

How to apply this?

⇒ Instead of worrying about your exam score, focus on consistent daily study.

⇒ Enjoy learning rather than just memorizing for marks.

⇒ Trust that hard work will always bring good results, even if not immediately.

Lesson 2: Control Your Mind to Control Your Life

उद्धरेदात्मनाऽऽत्मानं नात्मानमवसादयेत्।

आत्मैव ह्यात्मनो बन्धुरात्मैव रिपुरात्मनः॥

"One must deliver himself with the help of his mind and not degrade himself. The mind is the friend of the conditioned soul, and his enemy as well." (Bhagavad Gita 6.5)

⇒ The biggest obstacle to success is your own mind.

⇒ If your mind is disciplined, you can achieve anything. But if your mind is uncontrolled, procrastination, distractions, and negativity will ruin your progress.

How to apply this?

⇒ Start your day with positive affirmations: *"I am focused. I am disciplined. I am unstoppable."*

⇒ Avoid negative thoughts like *"I can't do this"* or *"I am not smart enough."*

⇒ Practice meditation or deep breathing to increase mental discipline.

Lesson 3: Failure is the First Step to Success

नेहाभिक्रमनाशोऽस्ति प्रत्यवायो न विद्यते।

स्वल्पमप्यस्य धर्मस्य त्रायते महतो भयात्॥

"In this endeavor, there is no loss or diminution, and a little advancement on this path can protect one from the most dangerous type of fear." (Bhagavad Gita 2.40)

⇒ Failure is a part of every great success story.

⇒ Every failure teaches something important and brings you one step closer to success.

⇒ Krishna says that hard work never goes to waste. Even if you don't see results immediately, your efforts will benefit you in the long run.

How to apply this?

⇒ If you score poorly in a test, analyze your mistakes instead of feeling demotivated.

⇒ Remember that even toppers have faced failures—but they learned from them and kept going.

⇒ Develop a growth mindset—see failures as opportunities to improve.

Lesson 4: Avoid Distractions and Stay Focused

विषया विनिवर्तन्ते निराहारस्य देहिनः।

रसवर्जं रसोऽप्यस्य परं दृष्ट्वा निवर्तते॥

"The embodied soul may be restricted from sense enjoyment, though the taste for sense objects remains. But, ceasing such engagements by experiencing a higher taste, he is fixed in consciousness." (Bhagavad Gita 2.59)

⇒ Distractions are the biggest killers of success. Social media, Netflix, useless gossip, and negative people drain your energy and time.

⇒ Krishna advises detachment from unnecessary distractions so that you can fully focus on your goal.

How to apply this?

⇒ Reduce your screen time—set a daily limit for social media.

Lesson 5: Surrender to Krishna and Be Fearless

सर्वधर्मान्परित्यज्य मामेकं शरणं व्रज।

अहं त्वां सर्वपापेभ्यो मोक्षयिष्यामि मा शुचः॥

"Abandon all varieties of religion and just surrender unto Me. I shall deliver you from all sinful reactions. Do not fear." (Bhagavad Gita 18.66)

⇒ Krishna assures that if you do your best and leave the rest to Him, He will take care of everything.

⇒ Many students doubt themselves, but having faith in yourself and in Krishna's guidance will remove all fear and self-doubt.

How to apply this?

⇒ Whenever you feel anxious, chant the Hare Krishna Mahamantra for peace and clarity.

⇒ Before starting your studies or an exam, pray for focus and strength.

⇒ Believe in yourself—you are capable of achieving great things!

Final Thoughts: Apply Gita's Wisdom in Your Life

The Bhagavad Gita is not just a book—it is a life manual for students, guiding you toward success, focus, and inner strength.

Key Takeaways:

⇒ Focus on your effort, not just results. (BG 2.47)

⇒ Control your mind to control your success. (BG 6.5)

⇒ Learn from failures instead of fearing them. (BG 2.40)

⇒ Avoid distractions and stay laser-focused. (BG 2.59)

⇒ Surrender to Krishna and be fearless. (BG 18.66)

If you apply even one of these lessons in your life, you will see a massive positive change. So, start today and watch yourself grow into the best version of yourself!

CHAPTER 21

LESSONS FROM THE LIFE OF LEGENDS

History is full of great personalities who have left behind powerful lessons for us. These legends faced hardships, betrayals, and struggles but never gave up. They remained committed to their values and goals, teaching us the true meaning of determination, leadership, and success.

Here are detailed stories of four legendary figures whose lives inspire us to remain motivated, disciplined, and fearless:

1. Sambhaji Maharaj – The Epitome of Fearlessness and Sacrifice

Incident: Sambhaji Maharaj, the courageous son of Chhatrapati Shivaji Maharaj, was captured by Aurangzeb and subjected to severe torture for over a month. Despite unimaginable physical pain, he was offered freedom in exchange for converting to Islam. Sambhaji Maharaj firmly rejected the offer, choosing death over dishonor. He stood by his principles and faith, even in the face of extreme suffering.

Lesson:

⇒ Stand fearless in the face of challenges.

⇒ Never compromise your values, even if it costs you dearly.

⇒ Mental toughness surpasses physical strength.

Application for Students: Just as Sambhaji Maharaj never yielded to threats, students should never surrender to fear, failure, or distractions. Stay determined in your goals, regardless of difficulties.

2. Srila Prabhupada – Unstoppable Determination and Faith in God

Incident: At age 69, Srila Prabhupada traveled to the United States with only 40 rupees and no support, aiming to spread the wisdom of the Bhagavad Gita. He faced poverty, illness, and rejection in a completely foreign environment. Despite these overwhelming challenges, he stayed firm in his purpose. Within just twelve years, he successfully established the International Society for Krishna Consciousness (ISKCON), spreading Krishna's teachings to millions worldwide.

Lesson:

> ⇒ Your determination, not your age or circumstances, defines your success.

> ⇒ Maintain unwavering faith in God while persistently working towards your goal.

> ⇒ Never give up, even if everyone doubts you.

Application for Students: If Srila Prabhupada could achieve global success at 69 despite severe hardships, students can certainly overcome their own challenges. Believe in your abilities and stay dedicated.

3. Maharana Pratap – The True Definition of Perseverance

Incident: Maharana Pratap lost the crucial Battle of Haldighati and was forced to retreat into the forests, enduring hunger, hardship, and betrayal. Despite receiving lucrative offers of wealth and peace from the Mughal rulers in exchange for surrender, Maharana Pratap refused to compromise. He lived through years of struggle until he eventually reclaimed his kingdom with honor and courage.

Lesson:

> ⇒ Temporary failure should never define your destiny.

> ⇒ True success demands perseverance, even when comfort and shortcuts seem tempting.

> ⇒ Self-respect and honor hold more value than wealth or power.

Application for Students: If Maharana Pratap endured years of hardship without giving up, students can persist through tough periods of study. Stay resilient after setbacks and never stop trying until you succeed.

4. Chhatrapati Shivaji Maharaj – Mastermind of Strategy and Leadership

Incident: Chhatrapati Shivaji Maharaj was a brilliant strategist and fearless leader. Trapped in Agra by Aurangzeb, Shivaji cleverly devised an escape plan by pretending to fall severely ill. Using large fruit baskets as disguise, he secretly escaped the Mughal surveillance. Once safely back in his territory, he regrouped, rebuilt his army, and later defeated the Mughal forces decisively.

Lesson:

⇒ Smart work is as crucial as hard work.

⇒ True leadership involves responsibility and intelligence, not just power.

⇒ Stay calm under pressure and find intelligent solutions to your problems.

Application for Students: Instead of blindly memorizing facts, adopt smart study strategies. Practice effective time management and prioritize important topics to achieve success.

Final Thought:

These legendary figures teach us to be fearless, determined, resilient, and intelligent in the face of challenges. Remember their lessons when facing your own struggles, and let their strength guide you toward success.

CHAPTER 22

LAST-MOMENT STRATEGY – THE POWER OF MOCK TESTS

"Only a Few Months Left – What Should You Do?"

I know, only a few months are left for your Entrance Exam. The pressure is high, time is running fast, and doubts might be creeping into your mind—"Have I done enough?" "Will I be able to score well?" "What strategy should I follow now?"

You will get a flood of advice from teachers, mentors, YouTubers, and toppers. Some will tell you to focus on revising notes, some will tell you to solve previous years' papers, and some will suggest studying for long hours without distractions.

But let me tell you one TOP STRATEGY—a strategy that can guarantee your growth if followed sincerely. A strategy that has transformed average students into toppers and given AIRs their final push to victory.

This is the Master Strategy for anyone who dreams of achieving an outstanding rank.

Success Is for Everyone – The Only Difference Is 'How Many Steps?'

Many students feel demotivated when they score low in mock tests or when they compare themselves to others who seem ahead in preparation.

But success is NOT reserved for a select few! It is available to anyone willing to put in the work. The only difference?

⇒ Some students need to climb just 2 steps.

⇒ Others need 10 steps.

⇒ Some may have to climb 40 or more steps.

But NO MATTER HOW MANY STEPS, EVERYONE CAN REACH THE TOP!

If you truly desire success and are ready to learn from your mistakes and improve, then NOTHING can stop you.

The Master Strategy – Fail Fast, Learn Faster, Succeed Before the Final Exam!

Most students make a huge mistake by waiting to feel "fully prepared" before attempting mock tests.

But here's the truth:

⇒ You will NEVER feel 100% ready.

⇒ The only way to become ready is to START NOW!

⇒ You don't succeed by avoiding mistakes; you succeed by fixing them quickly!

So, instead of studying endlessly and feeling "not ready," do this instead:

1. Take a Mock Test NOW. Don't wait. Just take it.

2. Analyze Your Mistakes. Find out why you lost marks.

⇒ Psychological Mistakes (silly mistakes, nervousness, time pressure).

⇒ Skill-Based Mistakes (lack of speed, poor time management).

⇒ Content-Based Mistakes (weak concepts, forgotten formulas).

3. Write Down Every Mistake in a Notebook. This will make you conscious of them next time.

4. Revise & Learn the Weak Topics. Don't repeat the same errors.

5. Give the Next Test. This time, avoid the mistakes from the last test.

6. Repeat Until Your Scores Skyrocket!

The Breakthrough Moment – Your Exponential Growth!

At first, you might still score low. But if you stick to this strategy, something magical happens:

⇒ Your mistakes reduce.

⇒ Your concepts become rock solid.

⇒ Your accuracy improves.

⇒ Your confidence grows.

⇒ Suddenly, you see EXPONENTIAL growth!

A time will come when:

⇒ Your gaps are filled.

⇒ Your scores jump drastically.

⇒ You start getting top marks effortlessly.

But this will ONLY happen if you persist! Have faith in the process.

Your Action Plan: No Fear, Just Test & Improve!

STOP WAITING. START TESTING.

⇒ You don't know how many steps you need to climb.

⇒ So don't waste time overthinking.

⇒ Start giving mock tests NOW!

⇒ Make mistakes FAST, learn QUICKLY, and fix them IMMEDIATELY.

The sooner you start this cycle, the sooner you'll reach success.

⇒ Your goal is NOT to give the final exam and "hope for the best."

⇒ Your goal is to ALREADY be at your peak BEFORE the final exam!

You are not preparing to "attempt" success. You are preparing to "GUARANTEE" it!

So, take action now. Give that test. Make those mistakes. Learn. Improve. And watch yourself transform into an AIR Ranker before the final exam even arrives!

CHAPTER 23

THE 3 LAWS OF SUCCESS

Success is not a mystery. It follows definite laws—laws that govern the journey of every achiever, every topper, and every champion. Once you understand and apply these laws, success becomes inevitable.

Here are the 3 Most Powerful Laws of Success:

1. Law of Attraction – What You Believe, You Achieve

Everything starts with a thought. Your beliefs shape your reality. If you keep thinking, "I am not good enough," or "I can't crack JEE/NEET," then you're already setting yourself up for failure.

> ⇒ But if you train your mind to think:
>
> > ⇒ "I AM an AIR Ranker."
> >
> > ⇒ "I AM improving daily."
> >
> > ⇒ "Success is already mine."
> >
> > ⇒ Then, your actions and environment will align to make it true.

Why does this work?

Because your mind will focus on opportunities instead of limitations. Instead of thinking, "This chapter is too tough," you will start thinking, "How can I master this?"

Action Plan to Apply This Law:

> ⇒ Start visualizing yourself achieving your dream rank.
>
> ⇒ Surround yourself with positive people and successful mentors.
>
> ⇒ Speak affirmations daily: "I am capable. I am focused. I am a ranker."

Your thoughts attract your results. So think like a winner!

2. Law of Action – Success Comes to Those Who Move!

Many students spend too much time thinking about success but too little time taking action.

Let me be blunt—

⇒ No amount of motivation will work if you don't ACT.

⇒ No amount of dreaming will work if you don't EXECUTE.

The biggest difference between those who succeed and those who fail is simple:

⇒ Successful students DO what others only THINK about.

⇒ They don't wait for the "perfect time." They just start.

How to Apply the Law of Action?

⇒ Give that mock test TODAY.

⇒ Solve that difficult chapter NOW.

⇒ Wake up and follow your study plan, NO EXCUSES.

Success belongs to those who take consistent, focused action. No shortcuts. No waiting. Just ACTION!

3. Law of Karma – Your Results Are the Consequence of Your Actions

This is the most powerful law of all. The Bhagavad Gita teaches us:

"You have the right to perform your duty, but you are not entitled to the fruits of your actions."

This means that your success is determined by your efforts, not by luck or external factors.

⇒ If you study with full focus, discipline, and sincerity, the results WILL follow.

⇒ If you waste time in distractions, no amount of prayers will help you.

⇒ If you plant good seeds (hard work, patience, consistency), you will reap good results.

How to Use the Law of Karma?

⇒ Focus on efforts, not just results.

⇒ Put in 100% without worrying about outcomes.

⇒ Trust that your honest efforts will bear fruit at the right time.

Karma is the only thing in your control. The result will take care of itself!

Conclusion: Success Is Now in Your Hands!

Apply the 3 Laws of Success:

⇒ Think success (Law of Attraction)

⇒ Take massive action (Law of Action)

⇒ Trust your efforts (Law of Karma)

If you believe in success, take action, and stay committed, you are already on your way to greatness.

Now, go and make it happen!

CHAPTER 24

LOVE MAKES LIFE BEAUTIFUL

I know many of you skipped other chapters and jumped straight to this one, right? **Good!** That means you already understand—**love is the most powerful force in the world.**

But let me ask you something…

How many of you love your parents?

All of you, right?

What can you do for them?

"Anything!"—That's what most of you will say.

But let's go a little deeper.

How many of you love your dreams and goals?

Hmm… not as quick to answer this one?

Why?

If you truly love your goal, you should be willing to do whatever it takes to achieve it—**not just when it's easy, not just when you're motivated, but even when the journey gets painful.**

Because **love isn't just a feeling.**

It's **a commitment.**

A Teacher's Love: Why Shri Sandipani Academy Exists

Most people start a coaching institute as a business. **For me, it was never about business.**

It was about **love.**

I see every student in my academy **as my own child.** I see their struggles, their dreams, their fears.

⇒ When I scold you, **it's not because I enjoy it—it's because I care.**

⇒ When I push you harder, **it's because I see the potential in you that you don't see yet.**

⇒ When I create extra activities like **additional classes, Sandipani Premier League, Performance Marathons,** it's not because I have to. **No other coaching does all this.** But I do it because **I refuse to let you settle for anything less than success.**

There are days when I fight with you, force you to study, remind you again and again of your dreams—sometimes more than your own parents do.

You may hate me for it now, but **one day, you will understand.**

Because **your real well-wishers aren't the ones who pamper you** and let you waste your time.

Your real well-wishers are the ones who **push you, challenge you, and even make you uncomfortable—just so that you can become the best version of yourself.**

Please, **don't make the mistake of losing the right people from** your life.

Don't fall for the wrong people who only tell you what you want to hear.

Do not spoil your life.

Now, let me share with you two stories of love—**one of a father, one of a daughter.**

Stories that will **change the way you look at love.**

Story 1: A Father's Last Wish—The Secret Behind Tata's First Car 🚗

When we think of **Ratan Tata**, we imagine a billionaire, a business tycoon, a man who built one of the world's most trusted brands. But behind his success, **there's a story of love** that very few people know.

It all began with **a promise to a father.**

One day, Ratan Tata saw a man riding a scooter in the heavy rain, his little son tightly hugging him from behind. The child was shivering, trying to hide his face from the cold wind. The father drove carefully, but he was visibly struggling.

Something about that image shook Tata. **He saw his own father in that man**—struggling, sacrificing, doing everything possible for his child.

That night, he couldn't sleep.

The next morning, he called his engineers and said:

"I want to build a car that every hardworking father can afford—so his child never has to shiver in the rain again."

Everyone laughed. **A one-lakh rupee car? Impossible!** No company in the world had ever built such an affordable car before.

But Tata didn't care. **It wasn't about business. It was about love.**

After years of struggle, criticism, and failures, **he did it.** The **Tata Nano** was launched—not as a luxury car, not to make profits, but to **honor every father who works silently for his children.**

Because **true love is when you see someone else's struggle as your own.**

Story 2: Arunima Sinha—A Mother's Silent Tears, A Daughter's Unbreakable Spirit ⛰️

Arunima Sinha was just like any other girl—full of dreams, full of life. She was a **national-level volleyball player,** ready to make her mark on the world.

Then came **the night that changed everything.**

She was traveling by train when a group of thieves attacked her, trying to snatch her gold chain. She refused to let go.

So, they **threw her out of the moving train.**

She crashed onto the railway track, and before she could move—**a train ran over her leg.**

She screamed in agony, but the night was silent. **No one was there to help.** Blood poured from her body as she lay there, helpless.

She tried to move. **Her leg was gone.**

For hours, she lay on the cold tracks, in unbearable pain, watching rats nibble at her open wound. **She wasn't sure if she would make it till morning.**

But someone was crying even more than her that night—**her mother.**

When Arunima was finally found and taken to the hospital, the doctors **had to amputate her leg.** The moment her mother saw her daughter without her leg, she broke down.

That night, as everyone was mourning the tragedy, Arunima looked at her mother and whispered:

"Maa, don't cry. I have lost my leg, but not my dream. One day, I will climb Mount Everest."

Everyone thought she was delirious. She couldn't even **walk,** and she was talking about **climbing the highest mountain in the world?**

But Arunima wasn't joking.

She trained harder than anyone could imagine. **She fell. She bled. She cried. But she never stopped.**

And finally, on **May 21, 2013,** the girl who once lay helpless on the railway tracks **stood at the top of the world—on Mount Everest.**

Her mother, who had once cried at her daughter's tragedy, now cried at her daughter's victory.

Because true love is never letting go of someone, even when the world tells them to give up.

The Lesson?

Love isn't just about relationships. It's about **how deeply you care for something.**

Whether it's your **parents, your dreams, or your future**—true love means **never giving up.** It means **sacrifice, commitment, and the willingness to push through** even when no one is watching.

This is the love I feel for you—my students.

You are not just numbers on a report card. **You are dreams. You are possibilities.** And I will never stop pushing you to become the best version of yourself.

So, tell me—

Do you really love your goal?

Then prove it.

Keep going, no matter what.

Because **love makes life beautiful, and it also makes dreams come true...** ♥

CHAPTER 25

MY SQUIRREL-LIKE EFFORTS TO HELP STUDENTS

Dear friend,

I want to share my heart with you—a message born out of pain, perseverance, and an abiding love for each one of you. I was given a second chance at life. After my third suicide attempt in 11th standard, I decided that if I was going to live, I would live for my country and its people. Back then, I had no clear direction; I struggled, I searched, and I failed many times until life slowly began to reveal my purpose. Today, my work is not just about running a coaching institute or a business—it is a mission to empower students, transform lives, and build a better future. Through every obstacle, doubt, and setback, I have never been alone. My best friend, Krishna, has always guided and supported me. I humbly request your prayers too, so that this mission reaches every deserving student.

Mission Prayag: The Triveni of a Complete Individual

Imagine the sacred Triveni Sangam, where the Ganga, Yamuna, and Saraswati meet—each symbolizing a unique quality:

- ⇒ Ganga represents purity and character.
- ⇒ Yamuna symbolizes devotion and surrender.
- ⇒ Saraswati signifies wisdom and competence.

I believe that to create complete individuals, all three qualities must coexist:

- ⇒ **Character** builds a generation that is honest, ethical, and principle-centered.
- ⇒ **Devotion** instills faith, resilience, and a higher purpose.

$\Rightarrow$ **Competence** ensures world-class education and skill development.

Our vision is not merely to produce toppers but to create future leaders of India—leaders who will transform society with their values, dedication, and excellence. This is Mission Prayag.

My Squirrel-Like Efforts to Help Students

In the great war of the Ramayana, while Lord Rama was building a bridge across the ocean, even a small squirrel contributed by carrying tiny pebbles to support the mission. Though small, that act was sincere—and Lord Rama recognized and blessed it.

Similarly, my efforts may not seem grand, but they come from the heart. Today, my coaching center makes a difference in one district of Maharashtra—Ahilyanagar—but my vision is much bigger. I dream of serving students across India, unlocking their potential, and helping them achieve their dreams. I know I am just a small squirrel in this mission, yet if each one of us contributes in our own way, we can transform education in our country.

A Small Effort, A Big Impact

Imagine a world where no child quits studying due to financial constraints. Imagine every student receiving the guidance and support they need to reach their true potential. This is not a distant dream—it can be a reality if we all contribute, whether by supporting a student, spreading this message, or simply praying. Every small effort creates a ripple effect that uplifts thousands.

Empowering Students Through Free Education

I want every student to know: if you have the fire to study, nothing should stand in your way. That is why we have created special batches for those who are truly passionate but held back by financial struggles.

⇒ **Free Education:** These students receive the same quality education as everyone else, without financial burden.

⇒ **Study Materials & Resources:** Uniforms, books, test series—everything is provided.

⇒ **College Fees Covered:** Financial limitations should never force you to give up on your dreams.

If you know any student facing financial hardships but eager to succeed, please connect with us:

⇒ Shri Sandipani Academy

⇒ Phone: 7501 988 988

⇒ Contact: Dr. Balraju Karri (Phone: 9325712963, Email: balraju.ssadirector@gmail.com)

My Heartfelt Gratitude

I am deeply grateful to many who have shaped my journey and supported me through my darkest hours:

⇒ I am extremely grateful to my Siksha Gurus, **HG Sundershyam Prabhu** and **HG Radheshyam Prabhu.** Sundershyam Prabhu filled my life with love and philosophical conviction, helping me withstand every challenge with the faith that Krishna knows what is best for me. Radheshyam Prabhu's visits to Shri Sandipani Academy reconfirmed that this mission was assigned to me by my Lord; his few words lifted me out of my despair.

⇒ I thank my parents for their unwavering support despite all odds—I love them dearly.

⇒ I thank **Srinivas Babai** and **Satyavathi Pinni,** who cared for me even more than my own parents when I needed it most.

⇒ I am grateful to my **Jija Sannyasi Naidu,** who stood by my family in Andhra while I was far away in Maharashtra, caring for my brother, sister, and parents with immense love.

⇒ I extend heartfelt thanks to my beloved wife, whose sacrifices have been my backbone, and to my **Sasu Maa and family**, who cared for us like the head of our family, ensuring my wife and children were always well looked after despite my busy schedule.

⇒ I remember my dearest friend, **Deep Mishra**, who is no longer with me but remains forever in my heart for his support during the foundational years of this mission.

⇒ I am profoundly grateful to the devotees of VOICE (Educational wing of ISKCON) who supported me at various phases of my life:

> ⇒ **Pawan Putra P**
>
> ⇒ **Kurmavatar P**
>
> ⇒ **Ratnadeep P**

⇒ In Ahilyanagar, I am deeply grateful to

> ⇒ **Laxminarayan P**, who stood with me when everyone doubted, blamed, and rejected me.
>
> ⇒ **Pankajnetra P** and his mataji, who cared for me like their own parents—I used to eat at their home when I was pennyless.
>
> ⇒ **Pugalia P**, with whom I stayed without paying rent.
>
> ⇒ **Raghavcharan P, Yogendra P**, and **Akash P**, who supported me during a phase when my health was at its worst and I was away from my family.
>
> ⇒ The devotee family of Rajamandry, who, without knowing me well, welcomed me into their home and fed me prasad daily with so much love.
>
> ⇒ **HG Girivaradhari P**, for engaging in services at ISKCON Ahilyanagar and trusting me, even though I felt unqualified.

⇒ I am thankful to my friend **Premvikas P**, who has always guided me and with whom I could share my heart in comfort.

⇒ Thanks to **HG Balagovind Prabhu**, who supported me like an elder brother during my darkest times

⇒ Thanks to my pillars **Nana Sir** and **Rahul Sir**, who are assisting my mission with high spirits.

⇒ I am grateful to my business coach, **Ameet Parekh Sir**, and his team, who are helping me grow my business holistically while keeping the spirit of service to humanity at heart.

The list is endless—I could write a book on gratitude alone. Without mentioning these names, I would not feel complete, for without all these well-wishers, I would not be who I am today. My Gurudev **HH Radhanath Swami Maharaj** always reminds me, "If you are not grateful, you are a great fool."

To all my well-wishers reading this section, forgive me if your name is not mentioned here. I remember each one of you, and I am always here to serve you in every possible way.

My Final Appeal to You

I have dedicated my life to this mission, but I cannot do it alone.

⇒ Pray that I remain strong in my purpose.

⇒ Pray that I never deviate from my path.

⇒ Pray that, when my time comes, I leave this world as a warrior—fighting till my last breath for this cause.

And if you ever remember me, remember me not as a teacher or an educator, but as a servant—someone who simply tried to light the path for others.

Thank you.